Happy, Healthy, Wealthy & Wise

Eric J. Safranek

AvanVive Publishing™
Orlando, Florida, USA
www.AvanVive.com

**Five percent of all proceeds from this book will be
donated to charitable causes all around the world!**

First Print Edition

ISBN-13: 978-1493564118
ISBN-10: 1493564110

CONTENTS

DEDICATION

This book is dedicated to my family y mi familia. To my mother Ruth who gave me a lifetime of love in just twelve short years; My father Earl who "finished my training" and taught me to "enjoy the ride"; my sister Samantha, my lifelong teacher, sounding board and therapist; mi mama Lilliam and mi papa Juan Alberto whom have provided all the encouragement, prayers and strength I needed to make this book a reality; and especially to my wife Paula who always believed in me, supported me and loved me, even when she knew I was wrong, crazy or just full of it! She took the time to understand me and for that I am forever grateful!

MESSAGE FROM THE AUTHOR

Happy, Healthy, Wealthy & Wise is the short and simple story of a typical person who is searching for answers and paths to improve their everyday life. Along their travels, our main character comes across a teacher who provides many lessons and much needed guidance in this quest towards betterment.

In order to allow my reader to imagine themselves as The Student and accept the possibility that anyone in our lives may be The Mentor, I chose to exclude the pronouns, "he" or "she" in this book.

As an author and a reader it has always been my belief that many books similar to this one simply offer a few basic concepts wrapped around a lot of "fluff." It is my goal here to get right to the point with as many useful and helpful concepts by interweaving them into this simple to read and easy to digest short story. No secrets, no hidden messages, but perhaps some allegory and symbolism mixed in if you so choose to read further in to the story.

I intend to provide my readers with the most steak and the least sizzle. I hope that you enjoy this journey, live these lessons to the fullest and flourish in success! Bon Appétit!

Eric J. Safranek
March 2013

Happy • Healthy • Wealthy • Wise

Our journey takes place
on the island of Isla de la Vida.

Vida is a beautiful tropical island
dissected by a vast mountain range
and abounding with peaks and valleys.

To the West lays the city of Vivre Mas
and to the East, the city of Vivre Mejor.

Today a frustrated student left the
fog and congestion of Vivre Mas
in pursuit of higher grounds
and greater perspectives…

Happy • Healthy • Wealthy • Wise

SUNDAY

After an hour or so of hiking up and down trails, our student finally reached a lonely summit and simply broke down. With tears streaming from the eyes, The Student yelled out, "Please! Please, help me! I can't do it anymore! I just can't keep going on like this!"

As if an answer to a prayer, The Mentor appeared and inquired what was wrong. The Student went on and on explaining how things hadn't turn out as planned. They complained about all the stress from work, and the utter discontentment in life…

The Mentor stopped The Student mid-sentence and simply said, "Change Your Thinking. Stop being so negative. Stop focusing on what you don't want. Stop stressing yourself out."

The Student wiped away the tears, took a deep breath and asked The Mentor to continue.

You can change your life the instant you change your thinking. There is nothing gained from negative, worrisome or stressful thinking. Learn to view each situation almost like that of a robot: without prejudice, without emotion, without fear. Remember this: YOUR life is based upon YOUR communication with YOURSELF. YOU create YOUR world. YOUR beliefs are what decide YOUR happiness, success, accomplishments and reality. Instead of looking for inspiration, decide to inspire others. Instead of praying for help, go to help others. Instead of searching for excuses, see the endless possibilities!

Get out of your comfort zone and try new things. Realize that there are no limits but the ones you set yourself. From this point forward, start thinking positive thoughts, of obtaining magnificent outcomes and living a successful life. As you do this, you will start to notice many coincidences. You will start attracting what you seek.

The Student pleaded with the mentor to learn more. The mentor agreed to provide a lesson a day for a fortnight as long as the student agreed to follow all the advice without question, meet up when and where the mentor determined and that The Student maintained that same tenacious will to learn throughout.

The Student agreed and they decided to get together again mañana at the next highest peak of the mountain range. They shook hands and parted ways as The Student began their journey back home.

LESSON 1
CHANGE YOUR THINKING

• You can change your life in an instant simply by changing your thinking.

• YOUR life is based upon YOUR communication with YOURSELF. YOU create YOUR world. YOUR beliefs are what decide YOUR happiness, success, accomplishments and reality.

• Positive thoughts open both the mind and the eyes to see what a negative mind cannot.

Happy • Healthy • Wealthy • Wise

MONDAY

The following day The Student arrived, out of breath and barely on time. The Teacher said that today's lesson should be obvious...Improve Your Health.

You've only got one body, one vehicle to get you through this lifelong journey, so take good care of it. It will get dinged, it will get bruised, and it might even break, but never stop improving it.

My grandmother once told me that it hurt to walk. Despite that, she continued to walk every single day because as she said, it is better to walk with pain than not to walk at all.

We exhibit one the most amazing mechanisms on Earth, our own physical bodies. From mending broken bones and building immunity to disease, to overcoming unbelievable disadvantages and adapting to new environments, we come to realize that our physiology is naturally holistic. Often our bodies will give us some not so subtle warnings when we neglect proper care of it. Fortunately, the human body possesses the capability of mending and curing itself.

Exercise truly is one of the primary building blocks of health and happiness. Regular exercise can reduce pain, stress and blood pressure while also fighting depression, increasing energy, improving strength and boosting self-esteem. The endorphins that are released during exercise boost your mood and simply make you feel better!

So...from this day forward, focus on living healthy. Eat what you like, just eat less of what is unhealthy or harms your body and more of what you know is good for you and increases your wellness. By lying to yourself you do no justice. The more honest you are at discerning what is beneficial to you, the better results you will attain.

Drink more water. Exercise both your body and heart every single day. Short term pain, long term gain. The better you treat your body today, the better your body will treat you tomorrow.

The Mentor then poured two cups of tea as they agreed to meet up at the next highest peak the following day.

Happy ● Healthy ● Wealthy ● Wise

LESSON 2
IMPROVE YOUR HEALTH

• Regular exercise can reduce pain, stress and blood pressure while also fighting depression, increasing energy, improving strength and boosting self-esteem.

• The last diet plan you'll ever need: Eat less of what harms your body and more of which benefits your body.

• The better you treat your body today, the better your body will treat you tomorrow.

Happy • Healthy • Wealthy • Wise

TUESDAY

On the third day, The Student was greeted with a question, "Who are you?" Confused, The Student looked for clarification only to receive two more questions, "What do you stand for? What type of person do you want to become?"

The puzzled look upon The Students face said it all. The Mentor went on to explain how important it is to first Define Your Morals and secondly to make sure that they align with your actions. The beliefs you choose to hold are up to you. If you do not take the time to decide which principals and morals you cherish most, how could you ever expect to possess them?

W.W.I.D. What Would I Do? This is the self-empowering, self-improving belief that you can make all the correct decisions and take all the same actions that the perfect version of you would choose. I know that I will always be led down the correct path if I follow my gut instincts and consistently make decisions that align with my morals. Every intelligent, sane person has a sense of right and wrong. When you break your actions down to the simplest denominator, you recognize that doing good things makes you feel wonderful and doing bad things makes you feel awful. This common sense approach to making your decisions will guide you along the correct path. Consistently following your most cherished beliefs will guide the general direction of your life's path towards becoming that person.

Take the time today to write down and describe the person you would like to become, the morals you wish to possess and the convictions you most strongly believe.

It makes no difference who you were yesterday. What you choose to do at this very moment is what matters most. Do not let your mistakes from the past define your future. It is through these mistakes and failures that life teaches us many lessons; what a shame that most of us only learn but a few of them. Remember that you can reinvent yourself in an instant, with a single decision and today is simply another day to get it right!

From this day forward, act like the person you've always wanted to be. If you are continually thankful you shall become more gracious. If you are consistently brave you shall become more courageous. If you are habitually kind and sympathetic than you will ultimately become more compassionate. Each aligned action is one step closer to becoming the person you strive to be. Do not allow your ego to deceive your heart. Allow your outward actions to mirror your inward essence.   Align your beliefs and transform your soul.

The mentor handed The Student a notebook and pen. They parted ways, agreeing to meet early the following morning at Serenità Beach.

LESSON 3
DEFINE (AND ALIGN) YOUR MORALS

● WWID – What Would I Do?

● Precisely determine what type of person you would like to become, the morals you would like to possess and the convictions you most strongly believe.

● Align your behaviors to mimic your morals and become the person you've always wanted to be.

WEDNESDAY

The Student arose just after sunrise and traversed the hills and valleys until finally reaching the southernmost point of the island and Serenità Beach. The Mentor was already there, sitting idle on the beach. As The Student stepped closer The Mentor said nothing, just tapped on the sand to signal The Student to sit down. Twenty minutes had passed before The Mentor uttered, "Reduce Your Stress."

The Mentor went on to explain, "Stress can weaken a body of any strength, impair a mind of any intelligence and sicken a body of any health."

Simply taking a moment to clear your mind may offer you all the salvation you seek. Concentrate on your breathing. In…out…in…out…in…out…

Learn how to meditate. Improve your patience and reduce your anxiety. Reconnect with nature. Go for a walk. Sit on a beach - literally or visually. Clearing your mind removes the clutter of indecisiveness, the weight of undue pressure and the infection of stressors. Concentrate on relaxing every muscle in your body.

Grab your bike and go for a ride. Clear your mind, get some fresh air and appreciate the abundance of beauty that surrounds you every single day. Turn up the radio. I know of nothing like music to instantly elevate or change moods.

Instead of focusing on something you can't change, focus on your passions. Change your state of mind from worry to motivation. Talk to others or simply write it down. Once you start sharing your worries and stressors, either with others or on paper, you will fine tune your concerns and discover what it is that is truly bothering you. Only by first identifying your problems with a clear mind can you then resolve them with decisive strategies.

Nothing else was said. They both just sat there for another twenty minutes starring off into the distance. They finally looked at each other and with a simple nod it was understood by both that they would meet again tomorrow, same beach, same time.

LESSON 4
REDUCE YOUR STRESS

- Breathe in...breathe out...

- Improve your patience, reduce your assumptions, and control your anxiety.

- Relax and reconnect with nature.

Happy ● Healthy ● Wealthy ● Wise

THURSDAY

As The Student returned to the beach, The Mentor asked, "Why do you wear such an expensive watch?" The student explained that they had seen many successful people wearing this same watch. "I thought you told me the other day that you didn't have enough money to get what you needed?" inquired The Mentor. The Student responded, "Well not everything I want or need."

People today have a problem prioritizing and living within their means. They will let their health suffer in order to buy something they don't need to impress someone they don't like while they work a job they can't stand. I cannot stress enough just how important it is to weigh and prioritize your Wants and Needs.

Abraham Maslow explained physiological and safety needs as: food, water, air, sleep, shelter and so on. Once these basic needs are met, we can be content, improve upon our basic needs or continue to surround ourselves with materialistic possessions. Now obtaining possessions themselves is not wrong, but keep in mind that the more things you own, the more these things will occupy your valuable time.

Experiences are more valuable than any house, car or personal possession that you will ever own, because experiences can never be taken away. They are actually the only things that you will ever truly own in life. Travel more, meet new people, share adventures, share great conversations and create amazing memories.

Take the time to decide what you truly need in life and how simplistically you choose to live. Write down and prioritize all of your needs and wants. By putting pen to paper one of two things will happen; either you will discover the abundance of your wants or the simplicity of your needs. Realize that if you have the power to purchase and read a book within the comfort of your own home that you are in the minority of the world population. Appreciate all your blessings however they may transpire.

Happy ● Healthy ● Wealthy ● Wise

LESSON 5
WANTS VS NEEDS

• Write out and prioritize all your needs and wants.

• Create memorable experiences.

• Appreciate what you have.

Happy • Healthy • Wealthy • Wise

FRIDAY

The sun finally arose over the cloak of the mountains as the two friends converged at the foot of Cresta Ridge. A shake of the hand, an exchange of a smile, and it was right down to business. "Today's lesson: Simplify Your Life."

Most people believe that life is complex…most people are wrong. Life is simple. We are born, we live, and then we die. The only thing that makes life complex is your interpretation of it. Have you ever heard the expression, "Ignorance is bliss?" Not to demean education, but it seems that the more we learn, the more we fear. The goal is to take your experiences and education then reincorporate that child-like happiness and endless possibilities to your current situation.

Once you relearn how to think like a child, you will see that riding a bike, going for a swim, or even enjoying a scoop of ice cream can become an extraordinary experience. The key is to enjoy the little things. Do one thing at a time and take pleasure from doing it, no matter what it is.

Always look to improve your life. Is there a better way that I could do this? Is there a more efficient way? Question everything you do in life and discover how you can operate more efficiently to give yourself more time to enjoy the little things. Do not be afraid of change. Learn to adapt to change in a world that is in a constant state of flux.

Avoid getting overwhelmed by information. With all the technology available to us today it is becoming increasingly difficult to differentiate between factual journalism and opinionated, unverified and untrustworthy stories. You must learn to look deep inside and see if you actually believe what you read before you "spread the fear." We are approaching a point in history where we will have to rely more upon what we **believe and feel** and less upon what we **see and hear**.

Once we learn to break things down to a simple denominator, we will see that life is not complicated. Things are neither good nor bad, they just are. Every external event is controlled and interpreted by the internal goings on between our own two ears. Every situation that we encounter can change, for better or worse, at any given moment. What we choose to focus upon is up to each of us.

And with that, they decided to meet up again the following day down in Vinho Valley, on the other side of the mountain.

Happy ● Healthy ● Wealthy ● Wise

LESSON 6
SIMPLIFY YOUR LIFE

• Think like a child, enjoy all the little things in your life and see the endless possibilities.

• Fear Nothing, Assume Nothing, Question Everything, Accept Change.

• Any situation can be improved in a moment simply by changing your thinking.

Happy • Healthy • Wealthy • Wise

SATURDAY

As the sun scorched down from directly above, The Student carried on, seeking the next rendezvous point deep in Vinho Valley. Upon arrival The Mentor handed The Student a ten dollar bill and declared that this was a reward for all their hard work. While first refusing it, The Student reluctantly accepted it, and then sat down.

"What are you going to do with this money" inquired The Mentor. The Student went on to explain how they had compiled a list of wants and needs in which there was something on their list that cost exactly ten dollars! The Mentor then asked, "How much money do you have?" To which The Student responded, "Well I now have ten dollars."

Shaking the head with disappointment, The Mentor then stated, "Today's lesson is: Save More Money."

I am proud that you have learned the lesson of wants and needs, but the next step is to free yourself from debt. Debt is like rain. It can drizzle at first, then quickly accumulate and finally flood. The two best ways to avoid these rainy days are by first reducing your debt and then building your reserves.

From this point forward, I suggest that you save at least ten percent of every dollar you earn and put it towards savings and investments. Put an additional five to ten percent towards charitable donations and helping others. Once you set this money aside you will notice that it is possible to live on less. It feels good to help those in need. Helping others will pay dividends to your soul, your karma and your overall well-being. I guarantee that you will never look back from your death bed and think to yourself; I should have made more money and helped less people…

Use less than twenty-five percent of your available credit and pay off your debts as quickly as possible. The smaller your obligations and the greater your capital, the more freedom and possibilities will exist in your life. Do not allow your debt to control your life's decisions. If repayment of your liabilities becomes your primary focus, then you will never truly reach your full potential.

The Mentor then asked The Student once again, "How much money do you now have?" To which The Student responded, "Eight dollars!" The Mentor smiled and nodded with approval.

Happy ● Healthy ● Wealthy ● Wise

LESSON 7
SAVE MORE MONEY

• Save ten percent of everything you earn and put it towards building capital.

• Set aside five to ten percent of your earnings towards charitable donations and helping others.

• The smaller your obligations and the greater your capital, the more freedom and possibilities will exist in your life.

Happy • Healthy • Wealthy • Wise

DOMINGO

It was a beautiful and sunny Sunday afternoon when The Mentor finally arrived at a quaint little café on the outskirts of Vivre Mas. The two shared a great conversation over a couple of espressos. After a while The Student admitted that it had been some time since they had shared such a great conversation. And with that, The Mentor went on to share the day's lesson: Develop Better Relationships.

The primary step towards better relationships is to first love yourself. For if you do not love, respect and appreciate yourself, how can you possibly expect others to do the same? Now I am not suggesting that you become a selfish, narcissistic, egomaniac. What I am advising is that you become less critical of yourself and appreciate everything you have to offer in each type of relationship in your life.

Next, build your team and stack the deck. I cannot stress how important it is to surround yourself with the right people. Just as the right spouse, business partner or friend will lift you to unparalleled heights, the wrong ones can sink you to unfathomable depths...or debts...

With all the technology available to us today, make sure to utilize it to its fullest potential. To think that you can now watch a recorded speech by some of our greatest leaders and motivators from anywhere in the world, all within the comfort of your own home, is nothing short of amazing! It no longer matters where you live or where you come from. You can surround yourself with the greatest minds the world has ever known and learn from the best in every field. Your team of mentors are simply awaiting your summons.

We all need to feel love and connection. Marriage may not be for everyone, but do not use that as an excuse to miss out on the opportunity to connect to as many human beings as possible. Do not be afraid to love and get hurt. Take chances with your heart, for you will recover faster from heartbreak than you will from regret. Appreciate loved ones while they are alive instead of waiting until the very last moment. Strong bonds, powerful friendships and intimate connections are what makes life worth living, so love with all your heart and remember that paradise can be found anywhere you have someone to enjoy it with.

So with a hug goodbye and a kiss on each cheek, they went their separate ways, agreeing to meet up next at The Great Northern Cliffs.

LESSON 8
DEVELOP BETTER RELATIONSHIPS

● Learn to love, appreciate and respect yourself.

● Surround yourself with the right people.

● Continually create strong bonds and personal connections with new people.

Happy ● Healthy ● Wealthy ● Wise

LUNES

The Student traveled to the northernmost point of the island. They finally came upon the convoluted and lofty cliffs overlooking the rocky waters below. With no one in sight, The Student followed the path eastward. After turning a bend, it became apparent; the next meeting was to take place at a cemetery along the cliffs, overlooking the ocean below. The Student grudgingly approached The Mentor.

"Isn't it beautiful? This is where I want to be buried once I shall pass" replied The Mentor. "I guess…" replied The Student, "I just always considered cemeteries to be kind of depressing." "Yes, it is sad, look at all this potential. How many people here died before reaching their full potential? How many dreams must have died with these people?"

"I brought you here today to remind you to Pursue Your Passions. If I were to ask you what you want out of life, would you even have an answer?" inquired The Mentor. Most people never really take the time to truly discover what it is that they actually seek. How can they ever expect to find it if they don't know where they are going, what they are looking for, or even if they are on the right track?

If you don't know what to do with your life, my advice is simple. Do things you've never done before, go places you've never gone and talk to people you have never met. People are your greatest resources. You will learn more from people then you ever could from any book or school. If you still can't find what it is that you seek, then create it. Invent a life that you are passionate about.

Once you get an idea of what you want to do, then ask yourself: if I did not earn a single penny from this endeavor, would I still be happy that I pursued this path? If your honest answer is no, then continue the search for your true passions. Now, what if money were no object? Where would you live, what would you do, who would you be with? Find your passion in work, life and love and you shall unearth your path to happiness!

Do not let life and career get in the way and distract you from what needs to be done today. I am telling you, the timing will never be perfect, but the best moment to start is RIGHT NOW! For every step forward is yet another step closer.

The Mentor then stood up and gave a palms-together bow, before walking away. The Student remained behind to reflect in solitary; comfortably surrounded by the serene and tranquil cemetery.

Happy • Healthy • Wealthy • Wise

LESSON 9
PURSUE YOUR PASSIONS

• Discover your passions in work, life and love and you shall unearth your path to happiness!

• Create a life that you are passionate about.

• Start **RIGHT NOW!**

Happy • Healthy • Wealthy • Wise

MARDI

Today The Student traversed hill after hill until reaching the grand plateau overlooking Vivre Mas. The mentor was sitting amongst the tall grass as The Student sat down to join in. The Mentor asked, "Do you enjoy your job?" To which The Student quickly retorted, "NO!" "And how much time do you spend at this job that you do not like?" asked The Mentor. "Sometimes as much as twelve or more hours a day…" tapering off as The Student was realizing the disgust within.

That is a problem with our society today; so few people are following their true passions. We waste our time working at careers that we are no longer interested in, or possibly were never interested in, simply to get by or just pay the bills. Working forty or sixty hours per week at a job you despise is not the secret to success. When you choose this path, there is always something missing from your life.

When you are not doing what you are meant to do then you are depriving yourself, your family and all of mankind. Maybe this is why it has taken us so long to evolve…a lack of moral and passionate leaders. Every single person on earth has the power to make a contribution to the human collective, what will yours be?

Most of us figure out as children what we want to be when we grow up, but toss those dreams aside with excuses of monetary compensation, lack of education or other self-defeating beliefs. We need to feed our passions. Maybe not as a full time career at first, but possibly on the side as a hobby. The more you pursue your passions, the more you will realize that it is not about the money. You would even do it for free simply to express yourself and share your passionate soul with the world!

Pursue your passions BUT be mindful of the opportunities and paths you may encounter along the way. Your passions may very well lead you towards something better than ever considered before. You will be amazed by the numerous opportunities that present themselves once you follow your heart. The timing will never be perfect, so don't waste your time waiting.

No job is perfect, but how we spend our time can always be improved upon. I am not telling you to go straight out and quit your job today. What I am suggesting is that you Reevaluate Your Profession and consider if you are on the right track or not. If not, then take well-coordinated and planned steps in the direction of your dreams. Obviously, we all have bills to pay. Do not ignore your obligations. Instead, as we say in Scuba, plan your dive and dive your plan.

"So we shall leave today with one final question to ponder," said The Mentor, "If time is our most precious commodity, how well do you manage your assets?"

LESSON 10
REEVALUATE YOUR PROFESSION

• Pursue your passions, express your true self and share your passionate soul with the world!

• Take well-coordinated and planned steps in the direction of your dreams.

• Time is our most precious commodity. Manage your assets wisely.

Happy • Healthy • Wealthy • Wise

MIÉRCOLES

The Student crept up the rain soaked mountainside, hacking through the overgrown terrain and fighting sporadic torrential downpours until finally reaching the precipice.

Subsequent to discovering a gleam of fire from a cave, The Student continued onward. Finally coming upon The Mentor who was in a deep meditative state, The Student sat down and followed suit.

Startled by a boom of thunder, The Student suddenly awoke from the meditation. The Mentor was already preparing some tea for the both of them and said to The Student, "You must learn to Increase Your Focus."

Remember that the task of sharpening an ax is not enough to cut a tree down, but every swing of the ax is yet another cut closer.

Can you cut a tree down with a dull ax? Absolutely!…but just like taking five to ten minutes to contemplate and focus your goals, sharpening the ax will save you much time and energy.

As you increase your focus, you shall improve your ability to pinpoint your goals. The three best ways I know to improve your focus is through meditation, contemplation and visualization.

Practice meditation. It should not be a burden, but a relief from the anxieties of the day. It may be practiced in as little as a few breaths in order to clear your mind, make an important decision or regain your composure. Relax and refocus. The best way to improve is to practice meditation on a daily basis. Consistent daily practice, even for a short period of time, will yield much greater results than longer sporadic attempts. Remember perfection is not the goal here, improvement is.

Once you clear your mind you can then: calmly work through problems; make better choices; and explore the endless possibilities. Contemplation is simply the minds way of studying without books. Once you are relaxed with a clear mind, take the topic of concern and focus only on that.

Lastly, learn to visualize with precision. Take your contemplation to the next step. Add sights, sounds, smells, tastes and textures. Live in your mind what you want to see in your life and so it shall be. See yourself accomplishing your goal, hear the crowd cheer, smell that ocean breeze, taste that fine champagne and feel those leather seats. Visualize your success and success will find you.

LESSON 11
INCREASE YOUR FOCUS

• Consistently practice meditation.

• Contemplate the endless possibilities.

• Visualize with precision. Live in your mind what you want to see in your life, and so it shall be.

GIOVEDÌ

Today the two of them met at the entrance of Macaco Canyon, on the south end of the island. They greeted each other and continued to walk through the passageway and farther into the gorge.

The Student started the conversation, "In the past I have tried meditation, contemplation, visualization and goal setting all to no avail. What am I doing wrong?" The Mentor responded with a question, "Did you really believe that you could attain your goals?"

There is a vast difference between simply wanting change and actually making changes. Mindless, scattered, unorganized thoughts, even positive ones, serve no purpose unless backed by the true belief that you will accomplish said task. **You must take the actions that will lead to your success.**

Just as you believe that ice is cold, and fire is hot, you must believe that you will succeed! Your belief must be that strong. Once it is, than you will start attracting all the good things that you deserve.

The failures that lead up to your success are there to provide you with the education, experience and motivation needed to accomplish your each and every goal. Your life is a perceived illusion. Most of our fears are not real. It is our preconceptions and experiences that form our reality. Our past is the filter by which we view the present. Take off your foggy sunglasses and see the unadulterated, unemotional and simplistic reality that we've all been personally diminishing with our self-defeating and often incorrect beliefs. Do not get discouraged by temporary setbacks. Instead, use it as motivation, learn the lesson, increase your focus and strengthen your determination.

Improve your confidence at every level. Believe in yourself, believe in your dreams, and believe in your success. Walk tall knowing that every step forward is a step in the right direction. Every failure is one more discovery of how to not accomplish your goal. Do everything you can to build your confidence in yourself for if you cannot believe in yourself or your dreams, how could you ever expect others to do so?

As their walk was coming to an end, the canyon opened up to a southwest view and that of a spectacular sunset usually reserved for postcards or movie endings. The Mentor advised The Student to go home and rest up, for tomorrow would be a strenuous day as they decided to rendezvous at Pinnacle Pointe, the second highest peak on the island.

Happy • Healthy • Wealthy • Wise

LESSON 12
BECOME A BELIEVER

• Just as you believe that ice is cold, and fire is hot, you must believe that you will succeed.

• Do not get discouraged by temporary setbacks. Instead, use it as motivation, learn the lesson, increase your focus and strengthen your determination.

• Believe in yourself, believe in your dreams, and believe in your success.

Happy • Healthy • Wealthy • Wise

VINERY

Friday started out bright and sunny as The Student departed upon the hike up the mountainside. When finally reaching the summit, there was no sight of The Mentor. The Student waited at the peak for nearly thirty minutes before The Mentor finally arrived and said, "I definitely am not as young as I used to be!" The Student jokingly responded, "So I guess today's lesson is not about being on time?" "No," responded The Mentor, "today's lesson is something you've been learning all along...Take More Action"

The Mentor went on to remind The Student about being out of breath at their first couple meetings. "Why do you think I paraded you all around this island?" asked The Mentor. "It was to show you how much improvement you can make in just two weeks simply by pushing yourself and taking more action. Now look at you. You are at the second highest peak on the island and as soon as we are done here, you are going to climb to the top of Monte Meta," as The Mentor pointed to the highest peak on the island that was now hidden by cloud cover.

The person I met back at that first summit was lost and looking for help. I have provided you with many of the tools for success, but what you do with them is up to you. I have shown you how to: mentally prepare, physically prepare, financially prepare, determine exactly what you want in your life, surround yourself with the right people, pursue your passions, fine tune your focus, and to truly believe in yourself and your future success. All of this is useless…unless you learn to accept it AND put it into action!

If you read one page a day, you will eventually finish a book. But if you increase your action by reading one chapter per day instead, you will reach your goal more quickly. More action leads to faster results. Legitimate, productive action…not just busy work. What steps can I take today to improve my tomorrow?

If a team only practices but never plays a game, how can they ever win a title? You may have the best ideas and incredible inventions, but if you are too afraid to risk failure and share them with the world, we shall never know. Risk is a part of our everyday life and I am here to tell you that the more strategic risks you take in life, the more success you will find. Remember, you are writing your success story every single day that you take a step forward in the right direction.

Do not let fear of failure cripple you from taking action. Most fears we face nowadays are simply negative mental rehearsals of failures from our past that we concentrate upon. Our fears that once served us so well throughout our evolution now hinder us. From this point forward, face your phobias, ignore your superstitions, conquer your fears and Take More Action!

"Well you better get moving if you are to conquer that mountain today" said The Mentor to The Student. "You will not be joining me?" inquired The Student. "No…this part of the journey you must face alone. This will give you the time you need to digest everything we have discussed. You can tell me all about it when we meet up tomorrow for the Lua Cheia Festival at La Playa de Vivre Mejor. Bonne chance!"

LESSON 13
TAKE MORE ACTION

• What can I do today to improve my tomorrow?

• The more strategic risks you take in life, the greater potential you will have of creating your own success.

• Face your phobias, dismiss superstitions, conquer your fears and Take More Action!

SÂMBĂTĂ

As The Student descended the final sand dune, they were greeted by the angelic beach and glorious festival below. There were tiki torches, bonfires and vivacious island music. Barbeque, fish fry and enough beer, wine and spirits to flood a small village. When The Student got closer they were surrounded by the beautiful people of Vivre Mejor. The Mentor greeted The Student with a joyous smile, a hug and a cocktail. "Cheers!" said the Mentor as they clinked glasses.

They wandered out to the end of the pier leaving the fiesta to continue behind them as the immense moon rose before them. "Be Happy Now!" said The Mentor. Have fun, celebrate, and laugh! Enjoy life! Do not allow your thoughts to snowball into negativity; instead, create positive snowballs from great thoughts and admirable actions.

Live with ENERGIA! Don't be the person that brings people down. Be the person that others want to be around. Let others absorb some of your great karma.

Do not take yourself or your life too seriously. Do not overthink difficult or trying situations. You'll have moments of weakness and moments of greatness, perfect moments as well as tragic moments, redundant stretches and flashes of enlightenment. Life is simply a series of temporary situations strung together. Life is simple: we are born and we will die. Your purpose on this earth is to make the most of what happens in between these two events. This will become your legacy. So make it count, make it memorable and create as many positive and wondrous moments as possible!

Practice what you preach and teach what you learn. For now I realize that I am both a child and an adult. I am both an apprentice and a teacher. I am both a student and a mentor.

"And with that, I believe it is now time for us to rejoin in the festivities! Santé!" Exclaimed The Mentor as they clink their glasses one more time.

The festival carried on, the music was booming and the beachside was packed. Locals and tourists alike were dancing the night away as they welcomed in the sunrise.

The two friends eventually parted ways, somehow knowing that it would not be the last time they would see each other. As The Student started ascending the hills to begin the journey back home The Mentor yelled out, "Vivir Mejor!" The Student turned, smiled and yelled back to The Mentor and the entire valley below, "Happy, Healthy, Wealthy & Wise!"

LESSON 14
BE HAPPY NOW!

• You were born, you will die. Your purpose on this earth is to make the most of what happens in between these two events. This will become your legacy.

• Only you can make you happy.

• Live with **ENERGIA!**

"A man becomes what he thinks about all day long."
-Ralph Waldo Emerson

"Believe nothing, no matter where you read it, or who said it - even if I have said it - unless it agrees with your own reason and your own common sense."
-Buddha

Happy • Healthy • Wealthy • Wise

AFTERWORD

It is my hope that you enjoyed reading this book as much as I did sharing it with you! I am proud to announce that I will soon be releasing the follow up book to Happy, Healthy, Wealthy & Wise which will take us back to Isla de la Vida for the next fortnight of lessons! As you pursue your dreams from this point forward, I now leave you with some parting words of advice to take with you on your journey:

We are all the authors of our own lives. Some of us write adventure, some write romance, yet others write tragedy. Some of our books are just more interesting than others. If your book is boring you, then write a new chapter and live what you want to read!

Keep living the dream and enjoy the ride!

~EJS~

To receive more information about
Happy, Healthy, Wealthy & Wise
as well as to purchase your
HHWW and AvanVive merchandise
please visit us at:

www.AvanVive.com

*Years from now, when you are old and grey,
what advice would you give to your eighteen year old
grand child?*

Share your wisdom with us and contribute to
one of my upcoming books by emailing your
answers to:

Legacy@Avanvive.com

RECOMMENDED READING

Think and Grow Rich
Napoleon Hill

The Magic of Thinking Big
Dr. David Schwartz

Mind Power
John Kehoe

The European Dream
Jeremy Rifkin

Who Moved My Cheese
Spencer Johnson

Unlimited Power
Anthony Robbins

The 100 Absolutely Unbreakable Laws of Business Success
Brian Tracy

The 4-Hour Work Week
Timothy Ferriss

The Secret
Rhonda Byrne

I Could Do Anything If I Only Knew What It Was
Barbara Sher

To purchase any of these books, please visit:
www.AvanVive.com

ABOUT THE AUTHOR

Eric J. Safranek was born in the suburbs of Chicago in what was at that time the small city of Naperville, Illinois. A few years after graduating high school from Lake Zurich, Illinois, he caught the "travel bug" and never looked back. These travels allowed him to not only backpack throughout Australia, but to also live and work throughout the US in: San Diego, California; Phoenix, Arizona; Copper Mountain, Colorado; Hilton Head Island, South Carolina; Savannah, Georgia; Fort Lauderdale, Florida and St John, USVI. Thanks to working at Club Med resort villages off and on for over ten years, he was able to live, work and play in: The Bahamas; Turks and Caicos; Dominican Republic as well as three stints in Cancun, Mexico including one final season in 2008 where he finally met his wife, Paula who is from Venezuela. Eric and Paula currently reside in Orlando, Florida where they are planning their next adventure… destination: Europe!

Happy • Healthy • Wealthy • Wise

www.ingramcontent.com/pod-product-compliance
Lightning Source LLC
Chambersburg PA
CBHW021436170526
45164CB00001B/266